Contents

Look for the **Thinking Cap**.
When you see this picture, you will find
a problem to think about and write about.

Li's favourite celebration

A special day

Li Shao lives in China. He lives
on a farm with his father, mother,
uncle, aunt and grandmother.

His eighteen-year-old cousin
Mei used to live with them too.
Now she lives and works in the city.

'I'm so excited. Mei is coming
home for the New Year **celebration**,'
Li told his best friend. 'I haven't seen
her for a whole year.'

Li knew that life was often
hard for people who went
to work in the city. There were
many questions he wanted
to ask Mei about the city.

celebration   type of party or other fun activity, usually organised because
it is a special time or something good has happened

Where the Money Is

Illustrated  Wang

China

My name is Sying. I live in Beijing, China. I am very lucky. My parents have good jobs, and I go to a good public school. In my city, there are many people who have come from the country to work in factories. Life for them and their children can be more difficult.

Li's mother and aunt are busy cleaning. They do this before New Year's Day. It is believed that cleaning before the holiday sweeps away bad luck.

New year's eve

Li woke early on New Year's Eve. He dressed and hurried
to the village to meet Mei. There she was! She was
hauling her bags off the bus. Li rushed up to help her.

'I'm so happy you're home,' Li told Mei. They walked
back to the farmhouse. Li told Mei that it had been
a hard year on the farm. The soil was poor. Floods had
ruined the crops.

'Thank you for the money you sent us,' Li said.
'We used most of it to buy food. It meant that I didn't
have to work on the farm. I could go to school.'

Mei smiled. 'I am very happy the money helps,'
she said. 'It's not much, but if you are educated, you will
have a better life. When you are older, you will be able
to get a good job in the city too.'

haul to pull or move something with extra effort

The Chinese New Year is also known as the Spring Festival. All workers in China get at least seven days off work at this time of year.

A family feast

At the farmhouse, Mei cried as she hugged everyone. She was very happy to be home. It had been difficult living in the city. She had been lonely and homesick.

In the city, Mei has a job in a shoe factory. She works long hours. She starts work at 8:30 a.m. and finishes at midnight. She gets only one weekend off each month.

That night, the family sat down together to have a special New Year's Eve dinner.

'I have missed everyone so much,' said Mei as they ate. 'But I'm happy to see that the money I send home helps our family. I'm glad Li is going to school.'

After the meal, they played *mah jong*, an ancient Chinese game. Everyone wanted to win, but it wasn't easy to build a winning combination of pieces. They all became so wrapped up in the game!

Time passed quickly until Mei looked up at the clock and realised that there was only a short time until the start of the new year – just five minutes!

Soon they were all counting down the last ten seconds together. They were happy that they had managed to stay awake to see the new year begin.

Like Mei, many **rural** people in China travel to the cities to find work. They work in factories, in shops, at building sites and in restaurants.

rural relating to the countryside; from the country

New year's day

Everyone woke early on the first day of the new year.

'I have a special surprise,' said Mei. 'I saved a little money and bought everyone a gift.'

Mei gave her family new clothing and shoes to wear. A few of the items she chose were red. Everyone was very happy.

'Wow, thank you,' said Li. 'This is the first time I've had new clothes to wear on New Year's Day.'

That night, the whole family walked to the local village.
They watched brightly coloured dragon and lion dances.
They laughed at the loud popping sounds of the firecrackers.

'The start of the new year is my favourite time of year,'
Li said, happily.

It is a tradition
for people to wear
new clothes on
New Year's Day. Red
is a traditional colour
for Chinese New Year.
It symbolises
good luck.

The lantern festival

The final day of the Chinese New Year ends with the
Lantern Festival. This year, the day of the Lantern Festival
was also Mei's last day with her family.

Both Li and Mei felt sad because Mei would return
to the city the next day. It would be at least another year
before they saw each other again. To cheer Mei up,
Li made two big, red lanterns.

That night, they took the lanterns to the Lantern Festival
in the village. There were many other colourful lanterns at
the festival. Some of the lanterns were shaped like animals.

'I will miss you when you go back to the city,' Li told Mei.
'But tonight, we can smile and enjoy the Lantern Festival!'

Put on your thinking cap

Write down your thoughts on these questions. Then discuss them with a classmate.

1. How do you think Mei feels about working in the city? What do you think she likes about it? What do you think she doesn't like?

2. Li knows that Mei pays for his schooling and many other things. How do you think this affects his feelings for his cousin? How do you think this affects how hard he works at school?

What's the issue?

China is changing. As with other countries, such as India and Vietnam, there are growing industries that provide more jobs than ever before. Most of the jobs are in cities. Many rural people are moving to cities to find work in factories. City workers often send a large part of their wages back home. While this is improving the lives of many poor families in rural areas, there are problems.

Some bosses take advantage of the many people who need jobs. Workers must work long hours for low wages. Sometimes bosses hold back wages. Sometimes they fire workers if they complain.

New year migration

More than 100 million rural people travel to and from Chinese cities. They go to the cities to work. Each Chinese New Year, most of them return home to their families in farming areas.

Chinese people living in other parts of the world also visit their relatives at Chinese New Year. Altogether, it is the biggest human **migration** on Earth.

migration   the seasonal movement of a group of people or animals

This postal worker is helping migrants send money to their families.

徐家湾邮局汇款代办点

Second class citizens

During the 1950s, China made a law that required people to **register** their family in the place where they live. People could get education, health care and other benefits only if they stayed in the place where they were registered.

In China, most people believe that conditions for people living in cities are better than for people living in the countryside. Many rural people have become migrants. They have moved to the cities to find work. However, they do not have the same rights as city dwellers, because they are not registered there. The Chinese government is now starting to change the laws to give migrants the same rights as people who are registered in the cities.

register to record details in an official document

Many young workers come to the city with a group from their village. They often live in sheds or small rooms lined with bunk beds.

Write down your thoughts on these questions. Then discuss them with a classmate.

1. There are more than 1.3 billion people in China. That is about one-fifth of the world's total population. Why do you think the government set up the registration system?

2. Now that the government realises that the system is unfair, it is slowly starting to change it. Why do you think this is a slow process?

3. How do you think city people in China might feel about the changing laws?

When migrants arrive in a city, they must first find somewhere to live.

Migrant families

When only one member of a family becomes a migrant, the family is split up for much of the year. Some migrant parents see their children only during the New Year celebration.

Other migrants travel to the city as a family. However, this also causes problems. Some migrant children cannot go to city schools. This is because they are not registered there or because their families cannot afford the extra fee for out-of-town students. Instead, they must go to private migrant schools. But these schools are often expensive, and they are not as well equipped as the state schools. In Beijing, some migrant schools are now being closed.

About 20 million children in China attend migrant schools in cities.

Keeping in touch

In 2005, China Telecom set up a service called Warm Hearted Phones for Migrant Workers. It provides video phones that allow migrants to see their families as they talk to them. The service helps migrants to feel less homesick.

Many small towns around the world are getting smaller. People are leaving because they think there is more work and better education in big cities.

Cities around the world

Escaping city crime

UNITED STATES – City crime is increasing in some US cities. Some cities have become so big in the last 50 years that many families have moved to the suburbs. Here they can have bigger houses and yards. This has made many city centres poorer and may have led to more crime.

The internet helps traffic problems

BANGKOK, THAILAND – In Bangkok, a three-kilometre (two-mile) journey can take up to two hours! Many rural people have moved to Bangkok to find work. The city has grown quickly. This has led to traffic jams and pollution. But a new website might help. It gives drivers up-to-date information about traffic jams. The police can use it to direct cars to roads with less traffic.

Improving neighbourhoods

SÃO PAULO, BRAZIL – Many people in big Brazilian cities live in slums called *favelas*. The homes are small and often unsafe. Some lack water and electricity. However, the city is working to give people ownership of the land they live on. It is helping them improve their neighbourhoods.

Slum problems

BARCELONA, SPAIN – Thousands of experts meet at the World Urban Forum, held every two years in different cities around the globe, including Barcelona, Spain. They discuss the problems of poor areas in cities, such as Rambla del Raval in Barcelona. About one-third of the world's city populations live in slums. Many people have little shelter or clean water.

What's your opinion?

Many factories in countries such as China, Indonesia, Mexico and Romania manufacture products for other countries because they offer goods at cheap prices. This helps their economy. Migrant workers from the countryside do much of the work. However, many of these migrants work very long hours and live in poor conditions.

- Should factories in these countries charge more for their goods? What could the factories do with more money?

- What is being done to help migrants? What else do you think could be done?

- Should all people be allowed to live and work wherever they choose? Why?

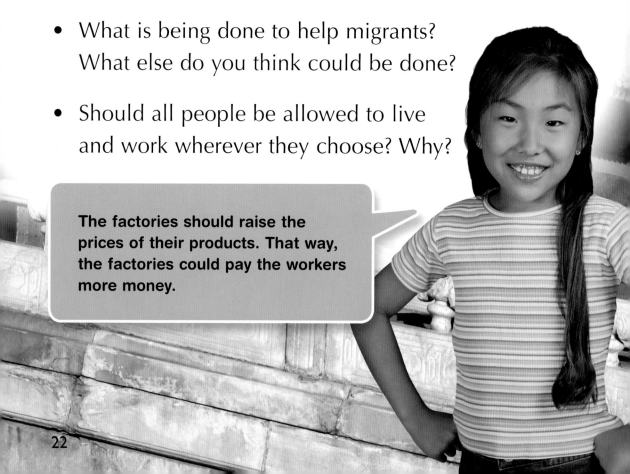

The factories should raise the prices of their products. That way, the factories could pay the workers more money.

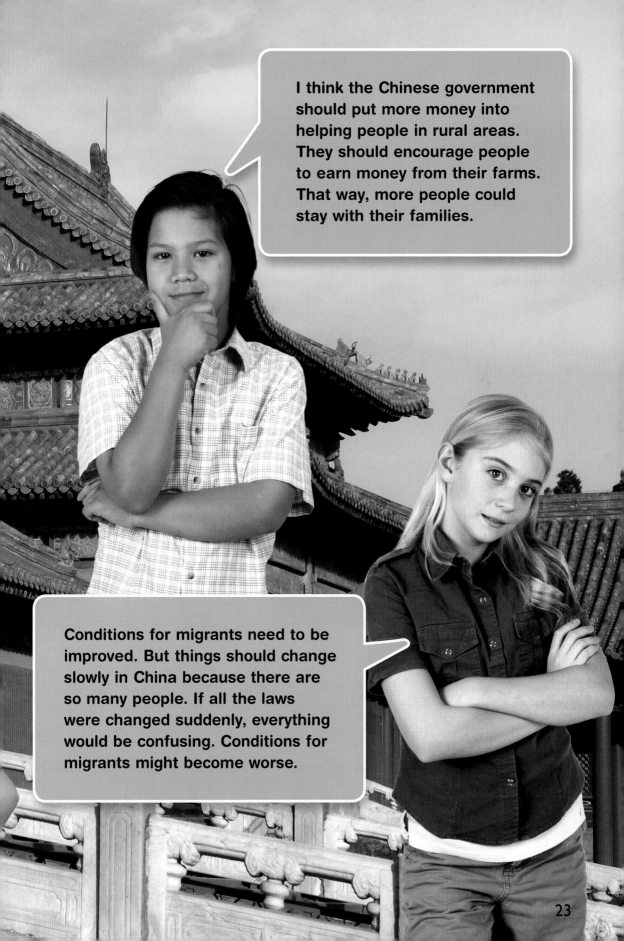

I think the Chinese government should put more money into helping people in rural areas. They should encourage people to earn money from their farms. That way, more people could stay with their families.

Conditions for migrants need to be improved. But things should change slowly in China because there are so many people. If all the laws were changed suddenly, everything would be confusing. Conditions for migrants might become worse.

Think tank

1 Around the world, more and more young workers are moving to cities. How do you think this affects rural communities?

Do your own research at the library, on the Internet, or with a parent or teacher to find out more about migration issues around the world and how people are working together to solve problems.

2 As cities get bigger, more housing and better transport are needed. What other things does a growing city need to plan for?

Glossary

celebration type of party or other fun activity, usually organised because it is a special time or something good has happened

haul to pull or move something with extra effort

migration the seasonal movement of a group of people or animals

register to record details in an official document

rural relating to the countryside; from the country